Supporting Language and Emotional Development in the Early Years through Reading

The invaluable 'Pip and Bunny' collection is a set of six picture books with an accompanying handbook and e-resources carefully written and illustrated to support the development of visual and literary skills. By inspiring conversation and imagination, the books promote emotional and social literacy in the young reader.

Designed for use within the early years setting or at home, each story explores different areas of social and emotional development. The full set includes:

- six beautifully illustrated picture books with text and vocabulary for each
- a handbook designed to guide the adult in using the books effectively
- 'Talking Points' relating to the child's own world
- 'What's the Word?' picture pages to be photocopied, downloaded or printed for language development
- detailed suggestions as to how to link with other EYFS areas of learning.

The set is designed to be used in both individual and group settings. It will be a valuable resource for teachers, SENCOs (preschool and reception), Early Years workers (nursery, preschool and reception), EOTAs, Educational Psychologists, Counsellors and therapists.

Maureen Glynn has 25 years' experience teaching primary and secondary age children in mainstream, home school and special school settings in the UK and Ireland.

Supporting Language and Emotional Development in the Early Years through Reading

Maureen Glynn

First published 2020
by Routledge
2 Park Square, Milton Park, Abingdon, Oxon OX14 4RN

and by Routledge
52 Vanderbilt Avenue, New York, NY 10017

Routledge is an imprint of the Taylor & Francis Group, an informa business

© 2020 Maureen Glynn

The right of Maureen Glynn to be identified as author of this work has been asserted by him/her in accordance with sections 77 and 78 of the Copyright, Designs and Patents Act 1988.

All rights reserved. The purchase of this copyright material confers the right on the purchasing institution to photocopy or download pages which bear the eResources icon and a copyright line at the bottom of the page. No other parts of this book may be reprinted or reproduced or utilised in any form or by any electronic, mechanical, or other means, now known or hereafter invented, including photocopying and recording, or in any information storage or retrieval system, without permission in writing from the publishers.

Trademark notice: Product or corporate names may be trademarks or registered trademarks, and are used only for identification and explanation without intent to infringe.

British Library Cataloguing-in-Publication Data
A catalogue record for this book is available from the British Library

Library of Congress Cataloging-in-Publication Data
A catalog record for this book has been requested

ISBN: 978-0-367-18835-1 (pbk)
ISBN: 978-0-429-35501-1 (ebk)

Typeset in Century
by Apex CoVantage, LLC

Visit www.Routledge.com/9780367136642

Contents

1. Aims and Learning Outcomes — 1
2. Target Readers and Users — 2
3. Using this Handbook — 3
   Rationale — 3
   Main Focus of the Pip and Bunny Stories — 3
   Four Ways to Present the Material — 4
4. The Six Illustrated Books — 6
5. Acknowledgements — 8
6. References — 9
7. Resources/Additional Ideas/Books for Each Story — 10

1. Aims and Learning Outcomes

The main purpose of these books is to develop the child's:

- communication and language development
- emotional and social skills.

Essentially, to:

- encourage enjoyment of reading and storytelling
- improve confidence for reading and comprehension
- widen vocabulary and generate ideas for story writing
- extend personal and social development awareness.

2. Target Readers and Users

The intended reader and user may be a:

- EYFS teacher in pre-school, mainstream or special school
- teacher of pupils learning English as another language (EAL)
- parent at home
- home school tutor
- speech therapist
- young child reader:
    1. Children in mainstream Pre-school or Reception Class/Year 1 settings will enjoy these stories with additional material/activities.
    2. Children experiencing special educational needs (SEN) will enjoy the stories and additional material, particularly with support for:
        - Emotional, Social and Mental Health (ESMH)
        - English as an Additional Language (EAL)
        - Speech and Language Therapy (SLT).

3. Using this Handbook

Rationale

The Department for Education, DfE, statutory Early Years Foundation Stage (EYFS) Framework states that of the required seven areas of learning development in Early Years settings, the following are of prime importance:

- communication and language
- physical development
- personal, social and emotional development.

To achieve the listed prime areas, children must be supported specifically through

- literacy
- mathematics
- understanding the world
- expressive arts and design.

https://foundationyears.org.uk/

Main Focus of the Pip and Bunny Stories

Mindful of the above framework, these books and additional material focus specifically on two of the three prime areas of learning, namely:

1. communication and language
2. personal, social and emotional development.

Four Ways to Present the Material

1. Simply as a picture story for listening and reading.

Six illustrated stories read by the teacher, therapist, parent or child will provide new material for imaginative enjoyment and confident learning.

2. As an aid to story writing skills.

These illustrated stories of everyday life, dreams, fantasy or adventure provide creative ideas for writing and art/craft work.

3. With What's the Word? picture pages* for language development.

The five pages of pictures, selected from each story, are offered for you to download onto a whiteboard or to photocopy and print in colour.

Each depiction provides a visual image to enhance language and observation skills.

It aims to extend vocabulary and build emotional literacy.

The five pages for each story illustrate:
- Action Words
- Location Words
- Descriptive Words
- Subject Matter Words
- Emotion and Feeling Words.

*The child offers words for the pictures, with help from the adult.

4. With Talking Points.

Suggested questions offered for discussion around the story aim to:
- encourage individual self-expression of thoughts, feelings and ideas
- help the child manage their feelings and how they behave
- improve self-confidence and self-awareness.

How to use What's the Word? picture pages

You may need to re-read or remind the children of relevant parts of the story first.

Your projection or photocopies of these pages can be used for group, individual or whole class work, depending on the number, interests and needs of the children you are working with.

How to use each of the Talking Points

Talking Points aim to encourage listening, comprehension, speaking skills and meaningful discussion.

They are story-based and relevant to the child's growing understanding of self and others.

Share each Talking Points question and ask the child/children what they think, feel or would do in that situation?

Talking Points may be used with or without What's the Word? picture pages.

4. The Six Illustrated Books

Book 1 *Pip's Dream*

Book 2 *The Flyaway Balloon*

Book 3 *Bunny Visits London*

Book 4 *Pip at the Seaside*

Book 5 *The Cheeky Ostrich*

Book 6 *Pip at Home*

Sequence for Reading the Books

Each picture story can be read by the teacher or child in any order, or followed as listed and explained here in this Handbook.

As there are a greater number of words in subsequent scripts, it might be preferable for the pre-school child and early reader to start with Book 1.

For each story this Handbook offers:

- the learning focus and general summary
- new vocabulary found within the text
- a four-step approach for delivery that includes:
    - 5 pages of extracted images for What's the Word? discussion
    - Talking Points for expression and comprehension
    - ideas for exploration of wider EYFS curriculum activities.

5. Acknowledgements

I would like to thank the following for their valuable input, encouragement and enthusiastic support:

My granddaughter, Ivy, and her toy Bunny who inspired these stories.

Ivy's parents Ben and Lois and other family members for sharing story ideas, photos and emotional support.

My husband William, for his beautiful photographs of sea gulls in flight and never-ending patience and care as I bounced off thoughts and storylines almost daily.

Routledge reviewers, especially the experienced Early Years Teacher.

Cassandra Pierson and her team, Speech & Language Therapist Service Lead – Essex.

Anne-Marie France, Speech and Language Therapist – Bradford.

Pat Kiernan, MA. Integrated Learning with Families and Children in the Early Years, Former manager of several pre-school settings in Co. Clare, Ireland.

Editors, Katrina Hulme-Cross and Emilie Coin at Routledge/Speechmark publications for their reassuring encouragement and much appreciated professional advice.

6. References

Government legislation for the Early Years Foundation Stage.

https://www.foundationyears.org.uk/files/2017/03/EYFS_STATUTORY_FRAMEWORK_2017.pdf

The Blank Language Scheme, highlighted by Cassandra Pierson, SLT Lead-Essex, for understanding the levels of language learning in early childhood.

7. Resources/Additional Ideas/ Books for Each Story

Book 1 *Pip's Dream*

Listening video of Peter and the Wolf on YouTube: https://www.youtube.com/watch?v=9ueGfjBKbiE

Book 2 *The Flyaway Balloon*

Making a kite: https://www.pinterest.co.uk/pin/103934703877341463

The Fantastic Flying Books of Mr. Morris written by W.E. Joyce, 2012

Book 3 *Bunny Visits London*

We're Going on a Bear Hunt written by Michael Rosen and illustrated by Helen Oxenbury

Books to enjoy about children in other countries:

https://delightfulchildrensbooks.wordpress.com/read-around-the-world/

Book 4 *Pip at the Seaside*

The Day the Sea Went Out, written by Margot Sunderland and illustrated by Nicky Armstrong

Book 5 *The Cheeky Ostrich*

Noah's Ark written and illustrated by Lucy Cousins

Animal craft ideas:

https://www.pinterest.co.uk/tonialgray/school-projects-animals-at-the-zoo

For Self-Expression:

A Trip to the Zoo written by Karen Wallace

DK Readers Level 1 https://www.penguinrandomhouse.com/series/KD1/dk-readers-level-1

Polar Bear, Polar Bear, What Do You Hear? written by Bill Martin Jr. and illustrated by Eric Carle

My First Reader: https://www.amazon.co.uk/slp/first-reader-books/7294dj68wmq87su

The Mixed-Up Chameleon written and illustrated by Eric Carle

Book 6 *Pip at Home*

Growing seeds and plants: https://www.earlyyears.co.uk/understanding-the-world/gardening

Pretend baking: https://www.nurseryworld.co.uk/nursery-world/news/1102998/baking

Role play people who help us:

https://www.earlyyears.co.uk/understanding-the-world/people-who-help-us

Book 1 *Pip's Dream*

Focus

In this story, Pip shows a range of emotions and feelings, such as attachment, loss, upset and anxiety, followed by the joy of finding and sharing an adventure with her special toy friend, Bunny.

The illustrations provide plenty of scope for discussion about feelings.

They will appeal to the child's curiosity and sense of fantasy.

The effect of light is presented in many forms to add interest.

Summary

Pip's dream will resonate with children who have a treasured toy that becomes their beloved friend and children who love forest adventure stories. It is magical, not scary.

The words and pictures lead us from the reality of loss, search and recovery, into the realms of fancy in Pip's dream. They aim to inspire the child's need for self-expression, creative activities and imaginative writing.

We follow Pip on her journey from sleeping and waking, loss and reunion, through to a woodland adventure with an unexpected surprise.

New Vocabulary/Script for

Pip's Dream

Pip loves Bunny.

This story tells what happened one night
Whilst Pip dreamt and the moon shone bright.

Pip and Bunny are asleep.
Suddenly there's a noise outside.

Pip wakes up.
She tosses and turns.
Turns and tosses.
Tosses and turns.
Oh no!

'Where's Bunny? Pip cries.'
Is she…

Under the duvet?
Under the pillow?
Under the bed?

'Ooh-ooh!
Where can she be?'

Pip creeps out of bed.

She looks in her wigwam.
But Bunny's not there.
Pip looks around her bedroom.

'There you are!'
Pip finds Bunny lying in the moonlight.
Sweet dreams Pip and Bunny!

As Pip sleeps, she dreams of a walk in the park with Bunny.

They come to a stile.

Where does that go to, Pip wonders?

They walk on…

Someone's watching!

'Listen Bunny.'

'Look up there!'

Deeper into the wood they go.

Suddenly!

In the clearing they find…

Not one, not two, not three

But seven bunnies all having fun!

Pip and Bunny enjoy a great time there.

Then they wake up.

Step 1 Listening and Reading

Read the story for enjoyment and to improve listening/ comprehension skills.

Step 2 Use the 5 Selected Picture Pages

Mindful of the above summary, project these selected picture pages onto a whiteboard or download, photocopy and print for sharing, to prompt ideas and provide additional vocabulary, to improve speaking and writing skills.

Step 3 Use Talking Points

Questions for the development of social skills and feelings of empathy.

Step 4 Progress to the Wider Curriculum

Optional links to the wider curriculum for extended learning.

These follow the Talking Points questions.

There are 5 What's the Word? picture pages for *Pip's Dream*.

Taking one page at a time, let the child offer you words for each image.

Action Words

Step 1

Read/remind the children about what happens in the story.

In the story, Pip sleeps peacefully and wakes suddenly.

She tosses and turns and searches for Bunny in her bedroom.

She talks to Bunny on their adventure through the park into the forest.

They find not one but seven bunnies singing and dancing to the music.

Step 2

Download/photocopy/print and share the action picture page.

Action Words?

Let the child tell you what actions the pictures convey.

Step 3

Use Talking Points to extend action words vocabulary.

Note:

Talking Points are for use with or without the pictures.

They are questions to prompt discussion and new vocabulary.

What action does Pip make in her bedroom?

What action does Pip make in her dream?

What do the bunnies do?

Do you sleep peacefully and have funny dreams?

What is it like to wake up suddenly?

What music do you like to sing and dance to?

Location Words

Step 1

Read/remind the children about what happens in the story.

In the story, the moon shines through Pip's bedroom window.

Pip looks for Bunny under the bed and in her wigwam.

In the park, Pip and Bunny climb over the stile, walk into the forest clearing and look up to the sky.

Step 2

Download/photocopy/print and share the location page.

Let the child tell you the names of each place they can see.

Location Words?

Step 3

Use Talking Points to extend place words vocabulary.

Name the place words used in Pip's story?
- under the bed
- in the park

- over the stile
- deep in the forest clearing
- up in the sky.

What do you see from your kitchen/bedroom/classroom window?

What might you see or hear:

- in the playground?
- in your local park?
- in the woodland forest?

Sound Words

Step 1

Read/remind the children about what happens in the story.

Pip hears the police car siren outside her window.

She cries when she wakes up.

Later, Pip and Bunny possibly hear an owl hooting in the wood and rustling leaves on the ground (suggested in the illustration but not stated in the script).

Eventually, they enjoy the sounds of dance music and singing bunnies.

Step 2

Download/photocopy/print and share the sounds picture page.

Let the child tell you the sounds each image conveys.

Sound Words?

Step 3

Use Talking Points to extend sound words vocabulary.

What sound words did you hear in the story?

Why was Pip crying when she woke up?

Where would you hear a hooting owl?

Do you enjoy dancing to music?

What is your favourite song or tune?

Light Words

Step 1

Read/remind the children about the story.

Pip is disturbed by the siren and flashing light.

When Bunny is missing, Pip eventually finds her on the moonlit bedroom carpet.

Pip and Bunny settle down to sleep again.

In her dream, Pip ventures out into the park at night time.

She can see clearly in the full moonlight but uses her torch on the pathway.

Pip shows Bunny the starlit sky.

They find all the bunnies singing and dancing in the moonlight.

As the dream ends, they wake up in daylight (not actually stated in the text).

Step 2

Download/photocopy/print and share the pictures of light.

Let the child tell you words for different kinds of light in the story.

Light Words?

Step 3

Use Talking Points to think about how we use light.

What looks different in daylight and at night?

Looking at the stars, what patterns do we see?

What shapes do we see in pictures of the moon?

Emotions and Feelings

Step 1

Read/remind the children about the story.

In the story, we know that Pip loves her Bunny but loses her in the bedroom.

Pip searches everywhere and eventually finds her lying on the carpet.

They go on an exciting adventure and enjoy a great surprise.

Step 2

Download/photocopy/print and share the page about emotions and feelings.

Let the child tell you how Pip feels at different times in this story.

Emotions and Feelings?

Step 3

Use Talking Points to explore awareness of self and others.

When do you feel loved?

Who do you love most?

How important are your friends and family?

When do you feel upset or angry?

What helps you feel better and calm?

If you lose a special toy, how do you feel about it?

- sad?
- lonely?
- jealous?
- unhappy?

If appropriate ask:

Has someone you know died? Or a family pet?

Who or what was it?

How do you feel about this loss?

Pip's Dream

Links to EYFS Curriculum Areas:

1. Expressive Arts

- Musical sounds:

  Use percussion instruments to create sounds that suggest rustling leaves, wild animals and small creatures present in the woods.

- If appropriate for your class/ child, download Peter and the Wolf to listen, act out or play instrumental sounds linked to characters in the story.

  https://www.youtube.com/watch?v=9ueGfjBKbiE

  It takes almost 28 minutes to run. Perhaps a small section might be sufficient.

- Paint a picture or make a collage of a woodland adventure story, or children playing in the park.

- Enjoy Anthony Browne's imaginative and inspirational illustrations in his picture story *Into the Forest*, published by Walker Books in 2004.

2. Role Play

Act out:

- Pip's search for Bunny in her bedroom.
- Pip's adventure through the park using torchlight and moonlight.
- Pip and Bunny's discovery further on.

3. Understanding the World

- Take an outing to your local woods to see, touch and understand the changing seasons of the year.
- Collect some leaves, barks and twigs to bring back to class.
- Name some of the trees you discover.

4. Communication and Language

- Encourage ideas and thoughts about forest adventures as found in:
  - *Red Riding Hood* – a Ladybird First Favourite Tales.
  - *We're going on a Bear Hunt* written by Michael Rosen and illustrated by Helen Oxenbury.
  - *Owl Babies* written by Martin Waddel and illustrated by Patrick Benson, published by Walker Books.

- Create a little picture story or poem about your own adventure in the woods. Think about what you see, hear, smell or touch in the woods.

5. Personal, Social and Emotional Development

Pip loves Bunny and is distraught when she can't find her.

Think and talk about:

- Love and loss of family members, friends, pets and toys.
- How we show we are afraid or angry or upset.
- What helps you to feel better and happy again.

Book 2 *The Flyaway Balloon*

Focus

In this story we focus on relationships and social skills.

Pip invites family and nursery school friends to her birthday picnic party in the park.

The invited family are uncles, aunts, cousins and grandparents.

Social skills involve her welcome for everyone, acceptance of gifts and the sharing of food, toys and party games.

Pip copes well with the loss of her balloon.

Summary

Planning a birthday party is exciting and fun.

Children look forward to going to parties or celebrating their own.

There is much to do to make everyone feel welcome on the day.

A picnic in the park allows space for running around, outdoor games and ride-on toys.

Helium balloons are tied to the canopy pole but one is released by Tommy and taken by the wind.

Pip is upset and needs Bunny.

Where the balloon flies to is left to the reader's imagination.

New Vocabulary/Script for

Pip and the Flyaway Balloon

It is Pip's birthday soon.
She wants to invite all...

Her nursery friends.
'Please come to my picnic party in the park. Pip.'

Her family...
Parents, uncles, aunties and cousins...
And her four grandparents.

On the day,
Mummy and Daddy and grandparents
Help to set up Pip's picnic party.

Pip says 'Hello' to everyone.
They have fun together and...
Pip blows out her birthday candles. But...

Tommy unties one of the balloons.
Oh! The wind is suddenly strong...

The balloon flies up high.
Higher and higher it goes.

'Where will it fly to, Bunny?' says Pip.

Step 1

Read the story for enjoyment, listening and comprehension skills.

Step 2

Mindful of the summary above, download/photocopy and share the picture pages to prompt ideas and additional vocabulary for speaking and writing skills.

Step 3

Use suggested Talking Points to develop emotional and social skills and an understanding of family relationships.

Step 4

Use links to the wider curriculum for extended learning and enjoyment.

There are 5 What's the Word? picture pages for *The Flyaway Balloon*.

Action Words

Step 1

Read/remind the children about the story.

Pip and Bunny watch all the preparations for the party.

Pip welcomes her guests.

She blows out the candles on her cake.

Pip cries for her lovely birthday balloon.

Hugging Bunny, they watch the balloon fly away.

Step 2

Download/photocopy and show What's the Word? pictures to describe what people are doing in the story.

Action Words?

Step 3

Use Talking Points to extend vocabulary and imagination around birthday celebrations.

Which words in the story tell us what people were doing?

Note: They often end with the letters 'ing'.
- writing the invitations
- preparing the food
- welcoming the guests
- playing games
- eating food
- blowing out the candles
- crying for the lost balloon
- hugging Bunny.

What did Pip do before eating some cake?

What did she do when the balloon flew away?

What would you do if the wind whisked away your balloon?

Location Words

Step 1

Read/remind the children about the story.

Pip's picnic party is in the park.

The park is very close to where she lives.

The balloons are tied to the canopy pole.

Food and drink is on a table under the colourful canopy.

Step 2

Download/photocopy and show What's the Word? pictures to name various places in the story.

Location Words?

Step 3

Use Talking Points for place words relevant to the child's world.

Which words in the story tell us about a place?

- in the park
- tied to the pole

- on the table
- up in the sky.

Where did Pip have her party?

What were the balloons tied to?

Where did the children play?

Where will the flyaway balloon go?

Birthday Words

Step 1

Read/remind the children about the story.

Pip is going to be three years old on her birthday.

She helps Mummy with her birthday invitations.

It will be a birthday picnic party in the park.

There will be presents and balloons.

There will be candles on her cake.

Step 2

Download/photocopy and show What's the Word? pictures to encourage use of celebration words.

Birthday Words?

Step 3

Talking Points about birthday celebrations.

What happens on your birthday?

Who helps you to celebrate your birthday?

Would you prefer to go out on your birthday or stay at home?

Have you been to a friend's birthday party? What did you do there?

What is the best birthday party food?

Family Words and Relationships

Step 1

Read/remind the children about the story.

Pip invites her friends and family.

Family are, her grandparents, uncles and aunties, cousins, Mummy and Daddy.

Pip does not have a brother or sister (sibling) yet.

Tommy is a nursery school friend.

Bunny is her comfort toy.

Step 2

Download/photocopy and show What's the Word? family and friends pictures.

Family/Relationship Words?

Step 3

Use Talking Points to think further about family, friends and relations.

Who did Pip invite to her birthday party?

Who were the children that came?

- nursery friends
- cousins.

Who would you invite to your birthday party?

Emotions and Feelings

Step 1

Read/remind the children about the story.

It is Pip's third birthday very soon.

She helps Mummy write the invitations for her picnic party in the park.

Pip welcomes her invited friends and family. They all enjoy a fun time together.

But Tommy unties one of Pip's balloons.

The wind catches it and it sails up high out of Tommy's reach.

Pip and Bunny watch it fly higher and higher in the sky.

Step 2

Download/photocopy and show What's the Word? pictures to explain the emotions felt by Pip and Bunny in this story.

Emotions and Feelings?

19

Step 3

Use Talking Points to explore feelings further.

How do you feel when inviting people to a party?

- nervous
- excited
- worried.

What makes you happy on your birthday?

- presents
- playing with friends
- being with family
- party food and cake.

How do you think Tommy felt when the wind took the balloon away?

- excited
- guilty
- anxious
- sorry.

What makes you feel sad, upset or angry?

Pip and the Flyaway Balloon

Links to EYFS Curriculum Areas:

1. Expressive Arts

- Draw and colour your favourite part of the story.
- Design and cut out some large colourful balloons, for a class picture with a cut-out balloon-man holding the strings.
- Use tissue paper, balsa wood and string to make a kite. See the suggested kite making ideas on the online Pinterest website. https://www.pinterest.co.uk/pin/103934703877341463

2. Role Play

- Act out a story that shows the effect of the wind:
  - walking to school on a windy day
  - clothes blowing on the washing line
  - boats tossing at sea
  - cruising along in a hot air balloon.

3. Understanding the World

Fly your hand-made kites in the playground or local park, on a windy day

How easy or difficult is this?

What else uses the power of the wind to work well?

- windmills to make flour that is then made into bread, pasta and cakes
- wind turbines to make electricity
- sails for boats and yachts to sail at sea
- giant waves for surfers to ride on
- flower seeds that blow elsewhere, such as dandelion seed parachutes
- aeroplanes and gliders for travel and enjoyment.

4. Communication and Language

Let the children express their ideas, read and talk about:

- birthday parties and games
- their own family and friends
- flying kites in the park or on the beach
- sailing in a boat
- balloons and hot air balloons.

Read: *The Fantastic Flying Books of Mr. Morris* written by W.E. Joyce, 2012

Borrow library books or purchase stories about flight for children to enjoy for themselves.

5. Personal, Social and Emotional Development

- How do you feel about very strong cold winds, sleet and snow?
- Would you prefer a gentle breeze on a sunny day? How does that feel?
- When is the wind useful and fun?
    - flying balloons or kites
    - whisking off hats and scarves
    - cooling us in hot weather.
- When is the wind dangerous and scary?
    - when it is a hurricane causing much damage
    - when it is a tornado lifting houses and cars
    - when it fuels forest fires
    - when it brings storms on land and sea.

Book 3 *Bunny Visits London*

Focus

The focus is on how we manage social and emotional feelings and show empathy.

The young listener/reader may choose to identify with Bunny and enjoy following her journey and adventures in London, as an imaginative story.

Alternatively, he/she may relate to Pip who is unaware that Bunny is away in London until she returns home from school that day.

Naturally Pip is anxious to find Bunny and is upset because she feels that she has lost her friend forever.

Only when Pip's father, Ben, comes home, is she reunited with Bunny.

The listener/reader is invited to reassure Pip that all is well, and to tell her all about Bunny's exciting travels and sights that day.

Summary

Bunny takes a ride to London in Ben's pocket, whilst Pip is in school.

Bunny enjoys seeing:

- many people travelling by train
- lots of toys in the toy shop
- red London buses, famous Big Ben, the London Eye and marching guards at Buckingham Palace.

When safely back home, the listener/reader (that is, the child) is invited to tell Pip all about Bunny's adventure.

To help you do this there are clues in the illustrations on the last page of the story.

New Vocabulary/Script for

Bunny Visits London

Whilst Pip is in school, her Daddy has a meeting in London.
His name is Ben.

He travels by train to Paddington Station. Bunny goes too.

Bunny enjoys the ride on the Underground tube train.
There are so many people.

In London, Bunny hops out of Ben's coat pocket
And spies a toy shop…

She has never seen so many toys and games to play with.
She hops and hops on, to visit the London Eye.
She takes a ride.
'Wheee, this is fun!' she yells.

Then Bunny hops onto a big red London bus.

She spots Big Ben and…

Watches the guards at Buckingham Palace.

Now it is time to go home.
Bunny has had a wonderful day!

Can you tell Pip all about Bunny's visit to London?

Step 1

Read the story for enjoyment, listening and comprehension skills.

Step 2

Mindful of the summary above, download/photocopy and share What's the Word? pages to prompt ideas and additional vocabulary for speaking and writing skills.

Step 3

Use suggested Talking Points to develop emotional and social skills around empathy as Bunny shares her wonderful experience to help Pip feel better.

Step 4

Use the links to the wider curriculum for extended learning.

There are 5 What's the Word? picture pages for *Bunny Visits London*

Action Words

Step 1

Read/remind the children about the story.

Pip's Daddy, Ben, travels to London with Bunny in his pocket.

Bunny enjoys the train journeys.

In London, she hops out of Ben's pocket and spies a toy shop.

She has never seen so many toys.

She takes a ride on the London Eye and the top deck of the London bus.

Upstairs on the bus she spies Big Ben.

She watches the guards marching at Buckingham Palace before returning home with Ben.

Meanwhile, Pip has been to school and come home to find Bunny not there.

When Bunny returns, Pip hugs her and listens to you (the listener/reader) telling Bunny's story about her adventure in London.

Step 2

Download/photocopy and show What's the Word? pictures to tell what Ben, Bunny and Pip are doing in the story.

Action Words?

Step 3

Use Talking Points to extend vocabulary and imagination about travel by train and an adventure in London.

What is Pip's Daddy, Ben, doing on the train?

- Working on his laptop and preparing for the meeting.

What is Bunny doing on the early morning train and the Underground train?

- Watching the other people who travel to London and looking forward to exploring.

What can you do whilst travelling on a train?

- look out of the window
- talk to your family
- read a book
- draw and colour your picture
- watch a video on an iPad
- play I-spy
- sleep.

What can you see and do in London?

Remind with examples for London as in the story:

- visit a famous place such as Trafalgar Square to feed the pigeons
- visit London Zoo
- go to a big store toy shop.
- take a boat ride on the River Thames
- meet with family or friends for a meal or special event.

What can you do in your nearest town/city?

Location Words

Step 1

Read/remind the children about the story.

Pip is in school.

Ben and Bunny travel by train and Tube into London.

Bunny visits the toy shop, rides the London Eye, hops on a red bus, spots Big Ben and sees the guards at Buckingham Palace.

Pip walks home from school with Mummy or Daddy, Nanna or Grandad.

Step 2

Download/photocopy and show What's the Word? picture pages to name places in the story.

Location Words?

Step 3

Use Talking Points to find place words relevant to the child's world.

Which words in the story tell us about a place?

- Pip's school
- on the London Eye big wheel

- on a London bus
- the Big Ben clock tower
- the guards at Buckingham Palace.

Note: If more appropriate, adapt the location questions and talk about specific places in your village, town or city.

Descriptive Words

Step 1

Read/remind the children about the story.

Describing words, or adjectives, tell us more about a person, place or thing to make something more interesting for the reader. Pictures are descriptive too.

Looking at the illustrations in the book we notice that:

- Ben wears a green and yellow scarf, and glasses.
- The lady sitting in front of him has a pony tail and reads her book.
- The man in front of her has a small beard and wears glasses.
- The lady in front of him is checking her phone messages.
- Bunny looks over Ben's shoulder on the first train and sits on Ben's knee on the underground train.
- The lady in a smart red suit wears earrings and glasses.
- The little girl wears a yellow hat with a green band, to match her yellow spotted green dress.
- The elderly lady, in the orange coat, has curly hair and wears glasses.
- There are plenty of descriptive images in the toy shop and cafe pictures.

Step 2

Download/photocopy and show What's the Word pictures to develop ability to describe people, places and things.

Descriptive Words?

Step 3

Use Talking Points for thinking and writing descriptive words.

Try to describe or tell us more about the people in the cafe?

Who can you see there?

- a mother and her two children
- her fair-haired daughter wears a green dress and hairband
- her smiling son, in the highchair, wears a red top and blue bib
- two women chat by the window seats
- sitting at the next table, a young man wears a red T-shirt and his girlfriend wears blue.

What are the shapes and colours you see in the toy shop?

- toy bricks
- a wooden train
- teddy bears
- soft dolls with big blue eyes and hair tied in pigtails, with red ribbons.

What would you like to see in the third toy-shop window?

Transport Words

Step 1

Transport words tell us how a person, vehicle or object travels from one place to another.

Read/remind the children about the story.

Ben and Bunny travel by the overland train and Underground Tube train.

The bricks in the toy shop are carried along on a wooden truck.

The toy engine train and trucks move along the wooden train track.

The big wheel of the London Eye carries people in glass pods.

Red double decker buses travel everywhere in London.

Step 2

Download/photocopy and show What's the Word? pages to improve knowledge of transport.

Transport Words?

Step 3

Talking Points for thinking and writing about how we travel.

How do you travel to nursery or school?

- by car
- by bus/coach

- by train
- by taxi
- by bicycle
- by plane/helicopter
- by scooter
- walking on foot?

How and where would you like to travel to?

- the park
- the zoo
- the farm
- London, Birmingham, Manchester
- another country
- the moon?

Emotions and Feelings

Step 1

Read/remind the children about the story.

Pip is not worried about Bunny during the day because she is busy at school and has friends to work and play with.

But she is worried when she is back home and Bunny is not there.

We know that Bunny will come back from London but Pip does not know this.

Eventually Daddy comes home with Bunny safe in his pocket.

The reader is invited to tell Pip all about Bunny's adventure that day.

Step 2

Download/photocopy and show What's the Word? pages to help explain the different emotions felt by Pip and Bunny.

Emotions and Feelings?

Step 3

Use Talking Points to explore feelings.
- How do you think Pip feels at school?
- How does Bunny feel when travelling to London and around the City?

- Is Pip worried when she gets home and Bunny is gone?
- What do you think she does?
- What would you do?
- How will Pip feel when you tell her about Bunny's visit to London?
- Have you lost something for a short time, or forever? If so, what was it and what happened?

Step 4 *Bunny Visits London*

Links to EYFS Curriculum Areas:

1. Role Play

Bunny travelled to London in Ben's coat pocket.

How would you like to travel to another place?

Talk about and act out your journey for a day outing or holiday.

- Where will you go?
- Who will go with you?
- How will you travel?
- What will you do when you get there?

Read and act out *We're Going on a Bear Hunt* written by Michael Rosen and illustrated by Helen Oxenbury.

It's great fun!

2. Understanding the World

Daddy Ben and Bunny travel to London on public transport.

Buses, trains and planes carry many people to where they want to go.

What other kinds of man-made transport are there?

- cars, lorries, vans and trams
- bicycles/trikes
- motorbikes
- hot air balloons
- scooters
- ships/hovercrafts/yachts
- planes/gliders
- spaceships.

How does each kind of listed transport work?

- by mechanical energy which makes for movement of machines to transport people
- natural energy from the wind and sea.

How do we get energy to help us move, walk and run?

- we eat food to give us energy and good health
- we breathe fresh air into our lungs
- we drink milk for strong teeth and bones.

3. Communication and Language

Within your class there may be young children from different countries and cultures who may be willing to talk about their way of life.

- Each child could bring in an object from home to talk about.
- Some children may want to share their experience of travelling to a different town, city or country during the school holiday.
- They could talk or write the story of how they felt about:
  - the journey
  - their arrival
  - the people they met
  - the place they stayed in
  - the food they ate
  - what they liked best.
- They might paint pictures to illustrate their story.
- This online site recommends lovely books to extend your child's learning about culture and customs in other countries.

https://delightfulchildrensbooks.wordpress.com/read-around-the-world/

4. Personal, Social and Emotional Development

Bunny has never explored London before.

Is she brave and adventurous?

Does Bunny worry and feel lonely?

- No, Bunny is a toy; she does not feel things like we do.
- She is brave and adventurous in the story.
- We tell Pip all that Bunny has seen and enjoyed.
- We reassure Pip that Bunny was safe all the time.

How did you feel when you visited your playgroup, school or new home for the first time?

- Worried, pleased, excited, lonely, happy?

Who helped you to settle in and feel happy there?

- Mummy, Daddy, teacher, assistant teacher, cousin, a new friend?

How could you help your friend, younger brother or sister, or a new child, settle into your playgroup, school or new home?

- show them where things are
- talk with them
- let them to join in your games and meet your friends.

Book 4 *Pip at the Seaside*

Focus

Developing social skills:

- Sharing creative activities such as making a sandcastle.
- Coping with disappointment when it is ruined.
- Fun play at the seaside.

Summary

Pip's grandparents live by the sea. Her cousins Joey and Anna live nearby.

On a sunny day she explores the rock pools with her cousins. They find interesting sea creatures, seaweeds, shellfish and a stunning seven-armed orangey-red starfish.

Later, they make a splendid sandcastle with help from the grown-ups. Together they fill the moat with sea water.

Disaster happens when an excited puppy comes running fast towards them. The bounding puppy can't stop and lands right on top of the castle itself.

Everyone laughs except Pip who is disappointed and cross. Daddy and Bunny give her hugs and comfort.

Eventually Pip cheers up and laughs too. Ice-lollies, splashing each other in the sea, shell collecting and drawing in the sand are great fun.

Back home at Nanna and Grandad's everyone is hungry. The cousins talk excitedly about their great day and tuck into a meal of scrumptious fish and chips.

New Vocabulary/Script for

Pip at the Seaside

One sunny day in Summer, Pip and Bunny visit Nanna and Grandad who live near the sea.

Pip's cousins, Joey and Anna, live close by too.

Joey wants to show Pip and Bunny his favourite place to explore, when the tide is out.

They run across the rocks and kneel to look into the clear pools of water.

They see spikey sea urchins, barnacles, shrimps, baby crabs and, under some seaweed, a beautiful, vivid orangey-red starfish with seven arms!

While Bunny takes a nap, Pip, Joey and Anna build a splendid castle made of sand.

Daddy puts a flag on the tall central tower and makes arrow slits in the turrets around the edge.

The cousins put on armbands to go paddling in the sea.

They have fun splashing each other.

Then they fetch their buckets to fill with water and...

Pour it into the moat surrounding the sandcastle.

'It looks like a real castle now!' says Pip.

But suddenly, an excited puppy comes running towards them...

The puppy can't stop... Oh dear!

He lands right on top of the castle and slowly sinks into the sand.

Everyone laughs because he looks so funny.

But Pip is cross and starts to cry.

She hugs Bunny and Daddy comforts her.

Mummy and Aunty Lucy buy ice-lollies for everyone.

Pip cheers up and laughs at the puppy too.

The children get dressed and look for sea-shells to collect on the seashore. They find...

Limpets, cockles, blue mussels, pearly oysters and tiny periwinkles.

Pip loves their different shapes and colours.

They place them in their buckets to take home.

They have fun drawing faces in the sand, using their spades and fingers to make the lines.

Back with Nanna and Grandad, Pip, Joey and Anna can't wait to tell them about their exciting day.

Then everyone enjoys fish and chips, sitting around the kitchen table.

Step 1

Read the story for enjoyment, listening and comprehension skills.

Step 2

Mindful of the summary above, download/photocopy and share What's the Word? pictures to prompt ideas and provide additional vocabulary for speaking and writing skills.

Step 3

Use suggested Talking Points to highlight emotional/social skills when creating something together and coping with the unexpected happening.

Step 4

Use links to the wider curriculum for researching rock pools and the seashore.

Learn how to keep safe at the seaside.

There are 5 What's the Word? picture pages for *Pip at the Seaside.*

Action Words

Step 1

Read/remind the children about the story.

Pip and Bunny visit their grandparents who live by the sea.

They play with their cousins Joey and Anna. They explore rock pools and find an amazing starfish.

Together, they make a sandcastle with help from the grown-ups.

They have fun splashing in the sea and filling the castle moat with water.

Following the ruin of their castle, the children laugh at the puppy, lick ice-lollies, collect sea-shells and draw pictures in the sand.

Back at Nanna and Grandad's they retell their day and enjoy eating fish and chips.

Step 2

Download/photocopy and show Find the Word picture pages to tell what Pip, Bunny, Joey and Anna are doing in the story.

Action Words?

Step 3

Talking Points to extend the child's vocabulary and imagination about all the fun things there are to do at the seaside.

What do the children and grown-ups make in the sand?

    – a castle with a moat filled with water.

What else do the children do at the seaside?

    – splash each other in the sea

    – laugh at the puppy

    – lick ice-lollies

    – collect sea-shells

    – draw pictures in the sand.

What does Bunny do while the children play?

    – she takes a nap in the sun and falls asleep.

What would you like to do at the seaside?

Location Words

Step 1

Read/remind the children about the story.

Pip visits Nanna and Grandad who live by the sea.

Mummy and Daddy and Bunny are with her. Cousins Joey and Anna live nearby.

They look into rock pools, play in the sea and collect sea-shells on the seashore.

They carry home their nets, spades and buckets filled with sea-shells.

Everyone enjoys fish and chips around the kitchen table.

Step 2

Download/photocopy and show What's the Word? pictures to name the places in the story.

Location Words?

Step 3

Use Talking Points to find place words from the story and other place words relevant to the child's experience or imagination.

Where do Pip's Nanna and Grandad live?

— near the sea.

Where do the children see the starfish?

— in the rock pool.

Where do the children find the sea-shells?

– on the seashore.

Where do they put the shells that they collected?

– into their buckets to carry home.

Where does everyone eat fish and chips?

– around the kitchen table in Nanna and Grandad's house.

Descriptive Words

Step 1

Read/remind the children about the story.

Describing words, or adjectives, tell us more about a person, place or thing to make a story more interesting for the reader /listener. Pictures can be descriptive too.

Looking at the illustrations in the book we learn that:

    It is a sunny day.

    Joey likes looking into clear pools of water when the tide is out.

    The cousins see spikey sea urchins and a vivid seven-armed, orangey-red starfish.

    They make a splendid castle, with a central tower, arrow slits and turrets around the edge.

    An excited puppy runs so fast that he can't stop and slowly sinks into the sandcastle.

    The children collect sea-shells, including tiny periwinkles on the seashore.

    They tell Nanna and Grandad about their exciting day.

Step 2

Download/photocopy and show What's the Word? pages to describe the people, places and things.

Descriptive Words?

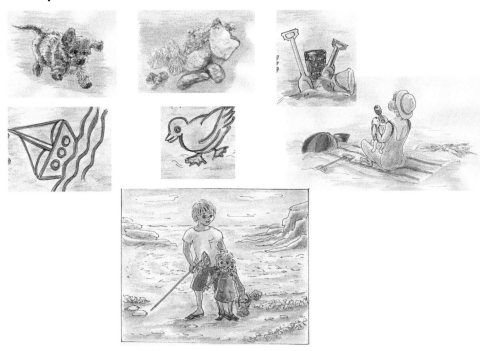

Step 3

Use Talking Points for thinking and writing descriptive words.

Try to describe or tell us more about:

- what Pip, Joey and Anna are wearing – the colours and shapes?
- what do they see in the rock pools?
- can you describe what the starfish looked like?
- what does the puppy look like?
- what do Nanna and Grandad look like?

Tell us about your cousins or your grandparents.

Do you get together sometimes for fun days at home or elsewhere?

Seaside Words

Step 1

Read/remind the children about the story.

Pip's grandparents live by the sea as do Pip's cousins, Joey and Anna. Joey loves to explore the rock pools to look for limpets, shrimps, cockles, mussels, baby crabs and sea urchins, hiding beneath the seaweed. He uses his fishing net to find them.

To their great surprise the children find an amazing starfish.

They use their buckets and spades to build the sandcastle and fill the surrounding moat with water.

They splash in the sea, collect shells and draw pictures in the sand.

Step 2

Download/photocopy and show What's the Word? pictures to think about the seaside things.

Seaside Words?

Step 3

Talking Points for drawing or writing about a day at the seaside.

You may have had holiday by the sea.

You may live near the sea.

Or maybe you can imagine what it would be like now that you have read Pip's story.

Who might go to the seaside with you for the day?

How will you get there?

What will you do when you are there?

- Will you sleep on the beach like Bunny?
- Have fun like Pip and her cousins?
- Will you take a picnic, eat at a cafe or eat when you get back home?

Emotions and Feelings

Step 1

Read/remind the children about the story.

We know that Pip loves her Mummy, Daddy and Bunny.

She also loves to visit Nanna and Grandad and play with her cousins, Joey and Anna.

She enjoys all there is to see and do at the seaside but is upset and cross when the puppy spoils their sandcastle.

Pip cuddles Bunny for comfort and Daddy gives Pip a hug to help her feel better.

Mummy and Aunty Lucy bring ice-lollies for everyone.

Pip cheers up and sees how funny the puppy looks, so surprised and flattened on the sand.

Step 2

Download/photocopy and show What's the Word? picture pages to explain how Pip feels in different parts of this story.

Emotions and Feelings?

Step 3

Talking Points to explore feelings.

How do you think Pip felt when first meeting her cousins at the seaside?

- not sure that they would like her?
- excited?
- happy?

How would Pip feel when exploring the rock pools?

- curious?
- afraid to look?
- brave/adventurous?
- wanting to see more?

What did she think when she saw the puppy running fast towards them?

- he's a cute puppy?
- I wonder what his name is?
- I would like to hold him?

What did she think when he landed right on top of their sandcastle?

- that puppy spoilt our castle?
- I don't like him anymore?
- I'm very cross with him?
- why is everyone laughing?

What would you do if a puppy or someone spoilt your sandcastle?

What would help to make you feel better?

What is it like when you meet other children for the first time?

How can you be friends together?

- say hello and smile
- join in games that you both like to play
- be kind to each other and share.

Step 4 *Pip at the Seaside*

Links to EYFS Curriculum Areas:

1. Role Play using props such as:

1. buckets and spades
2. fishing nets
3. arm bands
4. sea-shells
5. something soft (large cushions) to represent the sandcastle.

In small groups, choose one child to be the puppy, then act out:
- looking into rocks pools to see what you find there
- making a sandcastle together
- splashing in the sea
- puppy running fast and landing on top of the sandcastle
- licking ice-lollies and laughing
- collecting sea-shells in the buckets
- drawing shapes in the sand with a spade or your finger
- eating tasty fish and chips
- falling fast asleep.

2. Understanding the World

The effect of sea waves and safety by the sea.
- Set up a display table with objects and/or pictures relating to the seashore, such as:
- beach pebbles, sand and sea-shells, starfish and crabs
- bucket and spade and fishing rod
- beach towel, sunglasses, arm bands, sun cream and sunhats
- Let the children touch the objects and look at the images
- Talk about:
  - how the sea wears away rocks and stones to make sand
  - how sea-shells are washed in by the sea tides every day
  - how the rock pool is so clear as the tide refreshes the water each time
  - how we need to protect our skin from the sun's rays and strong breezes
  - how we need to wear armbands even when paddling in the sea
  - how to stay close to our family to keep safe all the time.

If possible, take the children to the seaside to experience the seashore and sea for themselves.

3. Expressive Arts

Make a group collage frieze of the seashore.

- Paint a large background of sky, sea and sand.
- Encourage the children to colour and cut out seaside picture shapes as shown in https://images.search.yahoo.com/
- Paste the shapes onto the background.

These might include:

- stones, pebbles and sea-shells.
- buckets, spades and fishing nets.
- children wearing sunhats and sunglasses at play.
- boats bobbing on the water
- seagulls flying high in the sky.

4. Communication and Language

Help the children to express their ideas, read and talk about other adventure tales and stories about the sea such as:

Billy's Bucket written by Kes Gray and illustrated by Garry Parsons.

Billy only wants a bucket for his birthday and no-one else is allowed to use it but of course Daddy does use it. The bucket contains wonderful sea creatures. This book is highly recommended on amazon.co.uk by both pre-school and Year 2 teachers who have built whole project work around this delightful story. This would make a fun idea collage too.

The Day the Sea Went Out written by Margot Sunderland and illustrated by Nicky Armstrong.

This story is for children who have lost someone they love. Over time, Eric makes a beautiful rock pool full of wonderful sea creatures.

What would you like to find in your bucket?

5. Personal, Social and Emotional Development

Unexpected things happen to us. We need to learn how to cope with them and know what helps to make us feel better.

References: *Pip at The Seaside* and *The Day the Sea Went Out* above.

Bunny fell asleep on the beach.

Can you tell Bunny about Pip's day at the seaside?

What happened at the rock pools?

What happened to the sandcastle?

Why was Pip upset?

What made her feel loved that day?

What can we do when we feel cross and upset?

Why does laughing make us feel better?

Book 5 *The Cheeky Ostrich*

Focus

Using fantasy and imagination for communication, language and visual literacy.

Enjoyment and laughter when something funny happens in a social setting.

Summary

Bunny wishes she could fly like Sammy seagull.

Sammy tells Bunny she can and Bunny is so excited.

They fly over the park, Pip's school playground, hills and lanes.

They land at the zoo.

Bunny and Sammy see many animals. They laugh at the funny penguins.

Then a lady waving her handkerchief has it plucked out of her hand and swallowed by a very cheeky ostrich.

The lady is shocked but everyone laughs as they watch the hanky slowly go down the ostrich's very long neck.

When it is time to go home, Bunny can't wait to tell Pip about her day.

Pip loves the ostrich story and laughs with Bunny.

New Vocabulary/Script for

The Cheeky Ostrich

    Bunny wakes up and sees
    Sammy seagull flying
    High in the sky.

    'Mmm…
    I wish I could fly,' sighed Bunny.

    'Of course you can,'
    Squawked Sammy as he
    Swooped down and
    Landed on the lawn.

    'Hop on my back and
    We'll go for a ride.'
    Bunny couldn't believe her ears.

    This was so exciting!
    On she hopped and up
    They went over the house,
    Over the park and over
    Pip's school.

    'Look!' cried Bunny.
    'I can see children in the park!'

    'Now I can see Pip's school!'
    'Children are running,
    Skipping, climbing and
    Playing hopscotch in
    The playground.'
    'Oh! There's Pip!' shouted Bunny.
    'Hello Pip! It's me, Bunny and
    Sammy, up here!'

But before Pip could look up,
They were gone.
Over the hills and lanes; down they
Swooped into the zoo.

Bunny sees lions, tigers
Zebras, leopards and
Giraffes; monkeys and elephants too.

'Look at the penguins,'
said Sammy.
'They are so funny as
They waddle around.'

Bunny spots a lady waving
A handkerchief to tell her
Friend where she is.

'Oh no!' exclaimed Bunny.
'You won't believe this!'

'That naughty ostrich
Has snapped up her hanky
And swallowed it whole.'

'Look! There it goes down
Its neck, bit by bit.'

The lady is surprised and shocked.
The crowd laugh.
'Well I never!' she says.
'What a cheeky ostrich that is!
Fancy eating my hanky, without asking.
No manners! That's what I say.'

Bunny and Sammy laugh too.
'Time to go home now,' said Sammy.

It was great flying today, thought Bunny.

'Thank you, Sammy,' she said,

As she slid off the seagull's back,

Safely onto the grass at home.

'I can't wait to tell Pip what happened today,' said Bunny.

Pip does enjoy Bunny's story

Especially when she hears about the cheeky ostrich.

She and Bunny laugh together.

Would you laugh too?

Step 1

Read the story for enjoyment, listening and comprehension skills.

Step 2

Mindful of the summary above, download/photocopy and share What's the Word? picture pages to prompt ideas and vocabulary for speaking and writing skills.

Step 3

Use suggested Talking Points to develop emotional/social skills to reflect how we might behave, when Bunny (that is, the child) tells Pip of her adventure that day.

Step 4

Use links to the wider curriculum for extended learning.

There are 5 What's the Word? picture pages for *The Cheeky Ostrich.*

Action Words

Step 1

Read/remind the children about the story.

Bunny wants to fly like Sammy seagull.

Sammy takes Bunny for a flight high above houses and the park and Pip's school.

Children are playing in the park and in the playground at school.

At the zoo, they see various animals and laugh at the funny penguins.

When a lady waves her hanky in the air, the cheeky ostrich swallows it and the crowd laughs.

When Bunny arrives back home, she tells Pip all about her adventure.

Step 2

Download/photocopy and show What's the Word? pictures to say what is happening in each action.

Action Words?

Step 3

Talking Points to extend the child's vocabulary and imagination.

What do you think it is like to fly over the rooftops on a seagull's back?

- exciting?
- frightening?

What did Bunny and Sammy seagull see in the zoo?
- penguins
- lions
- tigers
- zebras
- leopards
- elephants
- giraffes
- an ostrich
- lemurs.

What made everyone laugh?
- the ostrich slowly swallowing the lady's hanky down its long, thin neck.

Location Words

Step 1

Read/remind the children about the story.

Bunny and Sammy fly high over rooftops and the playpark, over Pip's school and down into the zoo.

Step 2

Download/photocopy and show What's the Word? pictures to name each place.

Location Words?

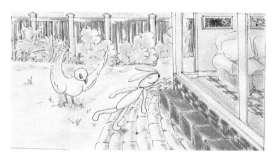

Step 3

Use Talking Points to find place words in the story and place words relevant to the child's experience or imagination.

Where does Bunny see children playing?

- in the park
- in the school playground.

Where do Bunny and Sammy find the animals?

- in the zoo.

Where does Bunny say 'Thank you' to Sammy?

- back in the garden at home where Pip and her family live.

Descriptive Words

Step 1

Read/remind the children about the story.

Describing words, or adjectives, tell us more about a person, place or thing to make something more interesting for the reader/listener.

Looking at the illustrations in the book we learn that:

Bunny wants to fly like Sammy seagull.

Sammy has broad wings and takes Bunny for a ride on his back.

We see rooftops, children playing, countryside and zoo animals.

Step 2

Download/photocopy and show What's the Word? pictures to improve ability to describe people, places and things.

Descriptive Words?

Step 3

Use Talking Points for thinking and writing descriptive words.

Describe or tell us more about:

- Bunny's flight with Sammy?
- The children in the park – what are they playing?
- The children in school – what are they wearing and doing?

Tell us about the lady waving her hanky.
- Why is the ostrich so cheeky?
- Why did the crowd laugh so much?

Zoo Words

Step 1

Read/remind the children about the story.

Bunny is visiting the zoo for the first time as the children may do.

The zoo keeps large animals, such as elephants and giraffes, from around the world.

The waddling penguins are funny.

The ostrich is cheeky for taking the lady's hanky and swallowing it whole.

Monkeys and lemurs love to climb and play all day.

Step 2

Download/photocopy and show What's the Word? pictures to find words for zoo animals and activities.

Zoo Words?

Step 3

Talking Points about the zoo.

Talk about the animals that Bunny and Sammy see.

What other animals/creatures do you think might be in the zoo?

- lions and tigers
- snakes and geckos
- cockatoos and budgerigars.

Why do we keep animals in a zoo?

- to learn about how they look after their babies
- to learn about what they like to eat and do each day
- to preserve them from harm and keep the species going.

What is your favourite zoo animal?

Tell us why you choose this one in particular?

Emotions and Feelings

Step 1

Read/remind the children about the story.

Bunny longs to fly.

She is so excited when Sammy offers to give her a ride and they fly over the rooftops, play-park and school.

She is so happy to see Pip playing outside in the school playground.

Bunny is surprised by the cheeky ostrich who stole the lady's hanky.

She can't wait to share with Pip all that happened that day.

Step 2

Download/photocopy and show What's the Word? pictures to explain Bunny's feelings in different parts of this story.

Emotions and Feelings?

Step 3

Talking Points to explore feelings.

How does Bunny feel:

- when she sees Sammy seagull flying high in the sky?
- when she is flying high over the rooftops with Sammy?

- when Sammy and herself watch the penguins?
- when she sees the cheeky ostrich swallow the lady's hanky?

How does Pip feel when she hears about Bunny's adventure?
- cross and annoyed that Bunny took such a risky flight?
- afraid that Bunny may have fallen and hurt herself?
- jealous that Bunny had all the fun and she did not?

Pip is smiling. Is she pleased and happy for Bunny?

How do you feel when your friend/ brother or sister have an exciting day without you?

When you are upset or jealous, what helps to make you feel better?

Step 4 *The Cheeky Ostrich*

Links to EYFS Curriculum Areas:

1. Understanding the World

Looking at how animals behave helps us to understand how we live too.

- Set up a display table with objects, books and pictures relating to the zoo, such as model animal shapes, animal stories and posters.
- Let the children touch the objects and look at the images.
- Talk about how animals live and look after their families.
- If possible, take the children to the zoo or a community farm to see animals for themselves, first hand.

2. Expressive Arts

- Read the story of *Noah's Ark* written and illustrated by Lucy Cousins:
  - to act out
  - to use as inspiration for paint or pastel art work.
- Google: Noah's Ark animal templates.

The printable black and white images are free to download.

- Make a collage frieze of some animals that went into the ark two by two.
  - Paint a long background of sky, seashore and stretch of sand.
  - Outline in black marker pen a large boat on the shore (see templates above).
  - Draw and colour some of the printed animal shapes using paints or pastels.
  - Cut out and paste the animal shapes onto the sand moving towards or onto the boat.
  - Add a rainbow overhead in the sky.
- Choose some animal craft ideas to make from pinterest.co.uk

  It might be:
  - animal masks
  - clay/Modroc animal models to create, paint and varnish
  - paper bag puppets

https://www.pinterest.co.uk/tonialgray/school-projects-animals-at-the-zoo

3. Communication and Language

Help the children to:

- express their ideas

- read for themselves
- talk about other adventure and zoo stories, such as we find in:

  A Trip to the Zoo author Karen Wallace.

  DK Readers Level 1

  https://www.amazon.co.uk/Trip-Zoo-DK-Readers-Level

  Polar Bear, Polar Bear, What Do You Hear?

  Author Bill Martin Jr. and illustrator Eric Carle

  My First Reader https://www.amazon.co.uk/

  The Mixed-Up Chameleon

  Author and Illustrator Eric Carle

  Picture Puffin

  https://www.amazon.co.uk/

There are many more to choose from online and in local libraries.

4. Personal, Social and Emotional Development

Nice things happen to our friends or family without us sometimes.

Other children may have something that we would really like to own or play with.

We need to learn how to cope with feelings of jealousy or anger and know what helps to make us feel better.

Bunny has such a wonderful day flying over the town with Sammy seagull and visiting the zoo.

Why was Bunny so excited to tell Pip all about what happened?

Pip listens and laughs at Bunny's story about the cheeky ostrich.

Do you think Pip wished she was there with Bunny too?

How do you feel when your brother/sister or friend has a toy or an exciting game/book/puzzle that you want to play with?

What do you do when this happens to you?

Book 6 *Pip at Home*

Focus

Coping with sudden unexpected physical pain.

Empathy with others who are hurting and in pain.

Summary

Pip and Bunny are happy at home and find plenty to do.

They love to read stories together and play hide and seek or dressing up with family and friends.

In the garden, they water the flowers and make a jug of petal potions.

Pip is badly stung by a bee. It really hurts. Daddy puts on magic cream.

Then her friend Tommy is stung by nettles. That hurts too.

She shows empathy and tells him that magic cream will make it better.

When helping to bake and washing her hands, Pip scalds her fingers under the hot water.

Finally, Pip enjoys a home-made flapjack and cuddles Bunny.

All is well again.

New Vocabulary/Script for

Pip at Home

Pip loves her home where she lives with
Mummy and Daddy and Bunny.
Their home is a terraced house.
Each door in the street is a different colour.

There is so much to do at home.
Pip loves to listen to stories with Bunny.
They look at the pictures and follow some of the words.

They play games indoors.
Pip knows all the best places to hide.
Mummy or Daddy count to ten slowly and then
try to find her.
Pip then counts and tries to find them.

Sometimes Pip and her cousins
or friends dress up.
They are beautiful princesses, a clever wizard
or a wicked witch…
A cruel pirate or a Red Indian running around the garden.

In the garden, Pip likes to water the flowers and
make petal potions in a jug.
Beside the shed, Pip suddenly screams with pain.
She screams and screams and cries.
It hurts so much!

Daddy carries her indoors.
'What's happened?' he asks.
Then he sees a nasty red sore on her leg.
'That's a bee sting!' he exclaims.

First he pulls out the sting with tweezers.
He soothes the sore with cold water and dabs it dry

Then he applies magic cream.

That will make it better!' he says, giving Pip a hug.

When Tommy falls over into the nettle patch, he gets stung too.

Pip wants to help.

She thinks and then she says to him.

'I know!'

"A dock leaf and magic cream will make it better!'

Today it is raining.

Pip helps Mummy to make flapjacks in the kitchen.

They use oats, golden syrup, butter and a few raisins.

Pip washes her hands because the syrup is so sticky.

But the water is too hot. Oh no!

She burns her finger. That hurts too!

Cold water helps to cool the pain.

When the flapjacks are baked and ready to eat,

Pip enjoys a square with Bunny.

It tastes delicious!

She feels much better now.

Step 1

Read the story for enjoyment, listening and comprehension skills.

Step 2

Mindful of the summary above, download/photocopy and share the pictures to prompt ideas and vocabulary for speaking and writing skills.

Step 3

Use the suggested talking points to improve emotional/social skill for coping with frightening pain and showing empathy to others in pain.

Step 4

Use the links to the wider curriculum for extended learning.

There are 5 What's the Word pictures for *Pip at Home*

Action Words

Step 1

Read/remind the children about the story.

Pip and Bunny listen to stories and look at the pictures.

Pip plays games indoors with her family and friends.

She waters flowers and mixes petal potions in the garden.

She helps Mummy bake the flapjacks and enjoys eating them with Bunny.

Step 2

Download/photocopy and show What's the Word? pictures to describe what people are doing in the story.

Action Words?

Step 3

Talking Points to extend vocabulary and imagination around home life.

Which words in the story tell us what Pip is doing?

Note: They often end with the letters 'ing'.

Pip is:

- listening to, looking at and reading stories at home or in school
- playing hide and seek and dressing up as a princess, wizard, witch, pirate or Red Indian
- watering flowers in the garden
- mixing petal potions
- baking and eating flapjacks in the kitchen.

Location Words

Step 1

Read/remind the children about the story.

Pip loves her home in a street of terraced houses.

She likes playing games indoors and helping in the kitchen.

She likes to be outside in the garden too.

There is a shed in the garden and a nettle patch.

Step 2

Download/photocopy and show What's the Word? pictures to name places in the story.

Location Words?

Step 3

Use Talking Points to find place words in the story and other place words relevant to the child's experience or imagination.

Where does Pip play hide and seek?

Where does Pip help to bake cakes and cookies?

Where does she get a bee sting?

Where do you like to play?

Where might you find a nettle patch?

Descriptive Words

Step 1

Read/remind the children about the story.

Describing words, or adjectives, tell us more about a person, place or thing to make a story more interesting for the reader.

Looking at the illustrations in the book we learn that:

    The doors in Pip's street are different colours.

    Dressing up is fun. You can be anyone you want to be.

    Petal potions are just a few different flower petals mixed into water, outdoors in the garden.

    Flapjacks are fun cakes to bake and even better to eat later, when cooled.

Step 2

Download/photocopy and show What's the Word? pictures to improve ability to describe people, place and things.

Descriptive Words?

Step 3

Talking Points for thinking and writing descriptive words.

Try to describe or tell us more about the houses in Pip's home street or your own home street.

Notice the doors, different windows and chimney pots on the roof.

What are the dressing-up games that you like to play?

Harry Potter witches and wizards?

Giant dinosaurs?

Clever doctors?

Police chasing robbers?

Busy shopkeepers and shoppers?

Scary trolls and goblins?

If you enjoy real or pretend baking and cooking, what would you like to bake?

Home Words

Step 1

Read/remind the children about the story.

At home we have different rooms for the different activities that we do.

Each room has different furniture inside.

Each cupboard, drawer or wardrobe holds different items.

Step 2

Download/photocopy and show What's the Word? pictures to improve knowledge of home activities and learn new vocabulary.

Home Words?

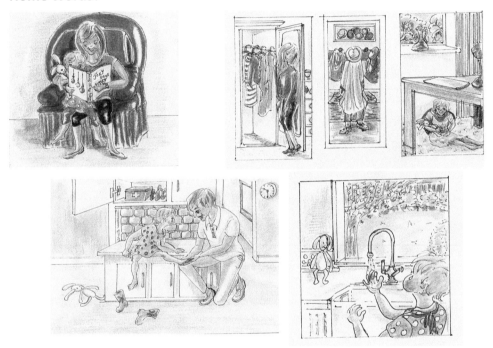

Step 3

Talking Points for discussion about rainy days at home or sunny days in the garden or park.

What can we do at home indoors when it is raining outdoors?

- play hide and seek
- dress-up and role play
- draw and paint

- watch children's TV or a DVD
- bake cookies or cakes.

What can we do outdoors when the sun is shining?

- play with sand or water
- help in the garden
- play in the park
- have a picnic.

Can you name all the rooms in your house?

- kitchen
- bathroom
- bedroom
- sitting room
- dining room.

Any other? Study? Cloakroom? Utility?

What might you find outside?

- a garage
- a shed
- a log store.

Where would you find:

- the oven and fridge/freezer?
- the washing machine and dishwasher?
- radio and television?
- car and bicycles?
- buggies and scooters?
- hats, scarves, coats and shoes?
- laptops, iPads and books?
- children's books, toys and games?

Emotions and Feelings

Step 1

Read/remind the children about the story.

We know that Pip loves her home where she lives with Mummy, Daddy and Bunny.

She also loves to play games with her cousins and friends.

She enjoys being in the garden too but is suddenly stung by a busy bee hiding in the grass. She is frightened as she does not know what happened and it hurts so much.

Daddy removes the sting and reassures her that magic cream will help to make her feel better.

Pip, in turn, reassures Tommy, who falls into the nettle bed, that he will feel better too.

When Pip is scalded by the very hot water she is less frightened but still hurting. She learns that cold water will help to cool the scald.

Step 2

Download/photocopy and show What's the Word? pictures to explain how Pip feels and reacts in different parts of this story.

Emotions and Feelings?

Step 3

Use Talking Points to further explore feelings

How does Pip feel when listening or reading a picture story with Mummy or Daddy?

- curious?
- bored?
- happy?

How does she feel when hiding in a good place at home?

- afraid to move?
- wanting to be found?
- excited?

Why does Pip cry when the bee stings her leg?

- she is frightened because the pain is so sudden
- she does not know what is happening
- it hurts so much
- she does not know what to do.

Are you upset by sudden noises?

- very loud music
- police/ambulance or fire service sirens
- thunder and lightning
- a howling wind
- loud bangs and fireworks on bonfire night?

Which sound frightens you most?

What helps to make you feel better?

Step 4 *Pip at Home*

Links to EYFS Curriculum Areas:

1. Understanding the World/Mathematics

Growing seeds and plants.

- Grow some cress seeds in half an egg shell or small yogurt pots.

https://www.earlyyears.co.uk/understanding-the-world/gardening

- Plant a sunflower seed in a small pot. When it is taller transfer it to a larger pot or plant it out in the garden. Measure how tall it grows. Is it taller than you?

Understanding water.

- Petals dropped into water will float but what happens when the water is stirred with a spoon?
- Find some plastic objects to put into a bowl or sink of cold or lukewarm water. Watch whether they float or sink. Does stirring the water make a difference or not?

Baking in class or at home.

- If appropriate for your children, try making real or pretend biscuits or flapjacks or jam tarts, in small class groups or one to one-adult and child/children.

Excellent advice here for pretend baking: https://www.nurseryworld.co.uk/nursery-world/news/1102998/baking

2. Expressive Arts

Role Play People who help us:

- Enjoy dressing up using hats, or tabards, occupation costumes or simple play trade tools and equipment.

https://www.earlyyears.co.uk/understanding-the-world/people-who-help-us

- Tell us who you are and what your work is all about.
- Act out a little story in small groups.

3. Communication and Language

Help the children to express their ideas, read for themselves, and talk about their own experience.

- Tell us who you would like to be when dressing up.
- What would you like to plant in a garden? How would you look after it?

4. Personal, Social and Emotional Development

If someone has chosen to wear the dressing-up hat, tabard or clothes that you want, what do you do?

- get cross, shout and stamp your feet?
- tell them it's yours not theirs?
- go away and sulk in a corner?
- say it's okay and let's take turns?

Have you ever been stung by a bee, wasp, mosquito or some nettles?

What did it feel like?

If someone is hurting what can you do?

- walk away?
- try to comfort them?
- tell your teacher or parents?

In Conclusion

If the six Pip and Bunny stories have inspired your teaching, and encouraged the children's enjoyment of reading and use of expressive language, then a great start to life-long learning has been achieved.

If the children are more confident in themselves, have learnt how to better cope with their feelings, understood the stories and tried some suggested activities, then good social/emotional progress has been made.

Sharing these stories with you has been a pleasure. I hope you enjoy them too.